Meditation & Art
Using Form to Connect with Your Essence

Meditation & Art
Using Form to Connect with Your Essence

By Ruth Platner, M.A.

Aperion Books

APERION BOOKS™
1611A S. Melrose Dr. #173
Vista, California 92081
www.AperionBooks.com

10 9 8 7 6 5 4 3 2
First edition published 2010
Printed in the United States of America

ISBN-10: 0-9829678-1-0
ISBN-13: 978-0-9829678-1-2
Library of Congress Control Number: 2010912743

Cover painting by Ruth Platner
Cover & book design by CenterPointe Media
www.CenterPointeMedia.com

DEDICATION

With gratitude to my magnificent personal family and
spiritual family, as well as friends
all over the world.

JOURNEY WITH ME . . .
There is a willow tree leaning towards the water. Walk
over there and sit under the shade of this lovely tree. Let
go of all tensions, stresses and worries. Feel saturated by
the calmness of serene surroundings.

TABLE OF CONTENTS

PREFACE

We have traveled a monumental distance from archaic, nature-based cultures through industrialized, materialistic societies, until today—where we are awakening to an integral consciousness which attempts to include all that was and looks toward to all that can be.

This can not be a solitary journey. We need to co-operate, shape and build upon each other's creativity. When we are in the process of creating together, we evolve. We manifest a new energy by expanding our consciousness. Together we can experience things that appear totally new. We become creators and co-creators.

Workshop participant Michael Mhead calls that, "Teaching your spirituality to walk." He adds, "The practical application for spirituality is: Act!"

The driving force behind the creation of this book was precisely that: Act. During my life of being an artist and art teacher, it has been my privilege to observe the process of unfolding and deepening of a kind of transcendental spirit in my students and fellow-artists. We are evolving…

This becomes increasingly clear when looking into the past. What has been learned? Remembering my early training at the Hamburg Art Institute in Germany—the struggle to get some feedback about my artwork from my teacher—a typically arrogant famous German professor of Art. The only indication of success was when he grabbed some of my drawings to hang in his office. I learned right there and then that I would become a different teacher. I would want to inspire. This lofty goal, in the course of time, evoked some practical inquiries about my function in this lifetime. The very short answer to this very complex question came back with stunning simplicity time and again: Your function is to be of service. To assist people who want to develop their infinite potential.

I decided to build upon this realization—hence this book. Evolution, both personal and cultural, is a fascinating topic for me. Does consciousness drive evolution or does evolution drive consciousness? If evolution were a moving vehicle, would we be the passengers or the drivers? In all possibilities, we might in turn be both. In any case, the awakening and broadening of our personal consciousness is as essential, as is the process of assisting our fellow humans in the evolutionary process, instead of leaving things to chance. Sometimes necessity creates progress of a sort. For example, the plague killed millions of people, thus shrinking the workforce. Thereafter, the industrial revolution replaced manpower with machines.

What does that mean to us now? We must stay very alert because our mechanized approach to contemporary life is driven by technology, which promotes the illusion of independence, thus separateness from each other. But, we are genetically social beings who wither in isolation. The necessity for community is becoming more and more evident. We are beginning to consciously form groups, where we come together with shared interests. We need each other. Seekers of emerging possibilities can support one another in the process of both, personal and social evolution. To include the entire planet—this is necessary!

I do believe that human beings have a drive for transcendence, hence the search for meaning which resides in the individual and extends to the universal.

This workbook is meant to benefit a variety of individuals and groups who wish to explore creative ways to celebrate life on this beautiful planet.

I believe the concepts and activities included are stimulating for children, seniors and also for veterans dealing with post-traumatic stress, as well as for the rest of us.

I would like to encourage readers to become leaders of groups. Feel free to share any of the activities in this book based on the universal principles listed and to add your own insights—Creativity!!!

As you will have observed from the listing of materials for each session, the cost is minimal. The creative mind is additionally stimulated when challenged to be inventive; i.e., to make something out of so-to-say: nothing. We used throw-away cartons, sticks, tree bark, paper, rags, etc. Some of the items were bought at the dollar store. Even the glass for the jewelry project can be replaced by pretty stone pebbles or shells. The potential for creativity is all around us; it is infinite.

INTRODUCTION

This is a manifestation book. It is based on the objective to demonstrate that meditation provides manyfold benefits.

The focus of this book is to enable groups of meditators to actively enrich their life-experience by gaining access to the energy of their centers of creativity. During meditation, we enter the realm of infinite possibilities. Here, all pre-judgment can be left behind and we can let creativity flow. Then, when we re-enter the ordinary–state in heightened consciousness, we are able to manifest an Art Project inspired by a specific Universal Principle—which we took into meditation.

Historically, we have become aware of the need for universal principles as foundation upon which to construct successful social systems.

The benefit of this process was expressed by some of the participants in the group we call: MEDITATION AND ART WORKSHOPS. They were pleased, sometimes surprised, by their artwork. They stated that looking at it periodically would re-connect them with the meditation experience which inspired it.

During the progression of the workshops, one could not help but notice how self- or outer-imposed limitations dissolved into self-acceptance and what emerged was the courage—even the need—to keep on creating artwork.

"WE DON'T SEE THINGS AS THEY ARE,
WE SEE THEM AS WE ARE."
—Anaïs Nin

~ S e s s i o n 1 ~
STAGES OF AWARENESS

Principle

Stages of Awareness.

Objective

To assess the effect of meditation.

Activity

Closed-eyed meditation and drawing.

Materials

Two sheets of 11 X 8 paper, soft pencil, colored markers or colored pencils.

Activity

Meditation, Drawing #1 & #2.

INSTRUCTION
PART 1

With closed eyes, place the writing utensil on any point on the paper. Start drawing simple lines expressing unedited feelings about the way your day went, the week went, etc. Your drawing should be nonfigurative (no recognizable forms such as dogs, people, etc.) You only need to express the way you feel. Do not look at the drawing. Put it aside, facing down.

GUIDED MEDITATION

Close your eyes and listen to the voice of a guided meditation: Sit comfortably and breathe deeply until you feel and enjoy the serenity and calmness of the moment. Now imagine yourself taking a stroll in the countryside. There are birds chirping, the fresh scent of flowers wafting towards you. Overhead the sky is blue with wispy clouds drifting by. You come upon a small brook. You hear the sound of water trickling over pebbles. There is a willow tree leaning towards the water. Walk over there and sit under the shade of this lovely tree. Let go of all tensions, stresses and worries. Feel saturated by the calmness of serene surroundings.

INSTRUCTION
PART 2

Now start drawing with your eyes still closed and feel the experience of the contact of the writing utensil with the paper. Go very slowly and let the movement of your hand be guided by the serene condition of your being. Put your pencil down and open your eyes.

DISCUSSION

Everyone compares their own two drawings, the one before the meditation and the one after the meditation. Examine and discuss how they differ. Avoid making value judgments of the two drawings; simply acknowledge the difference between them.

To enhance your expressions, you can use color pencils or markers and think about the emotional impact of colors.

CLOSING MEDITATION

Close your eyes and allow your body to relax deeply: From the top of your head to your shoulders, your back, your torso to your legs and your feet. Breathe deeply and evenly while in your mind's eye you review your two drawings. Affirm the difference between them. Recall your second drawing and enjoy the soft, gentle lines you drew in the state of meditative relaxation.

The metaphor for this meditation is: that you brought with you to this gathering a tightly wrapped package. Meditating gave you time and courage to unwrap it and view the contents, even let them spill out to reveal their surprising beauty–revealing the soothing liquid forms you translated into a piece of art. You have demonstrated to yourself that you can use meditation to transform states of tension to the blessing of openness where you can allow your creativity to flow. Here you can gain new insights into your self and your purpose. Meditation unveiled your ability to manifest. Thank yourself. Open your eyes and thank everybody for sharing this experience.

Before Meditation - Mari Shurian

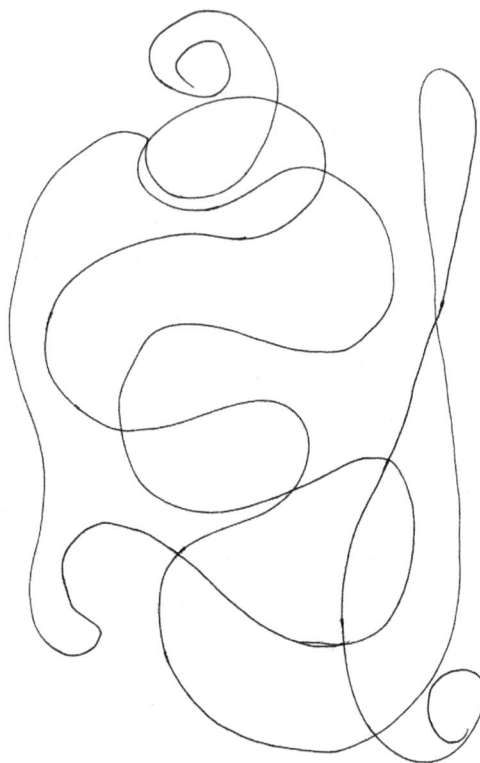

After Meditation - Mari Shurian

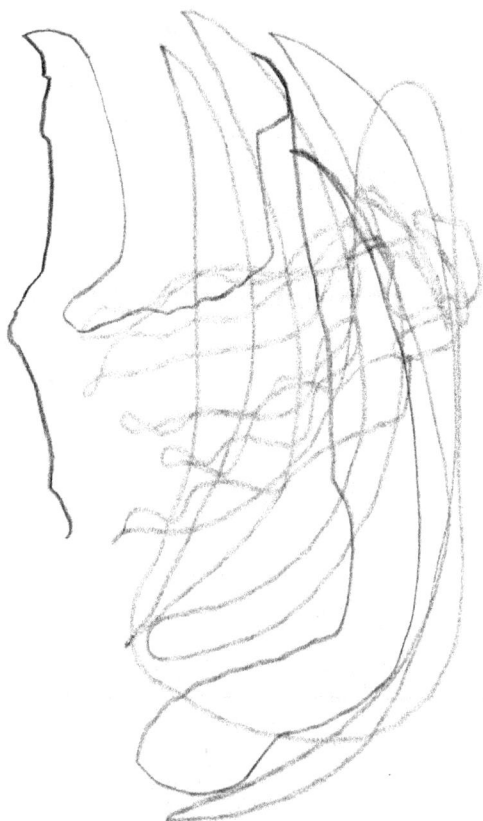

Before Meditation - Coty Benrimoj

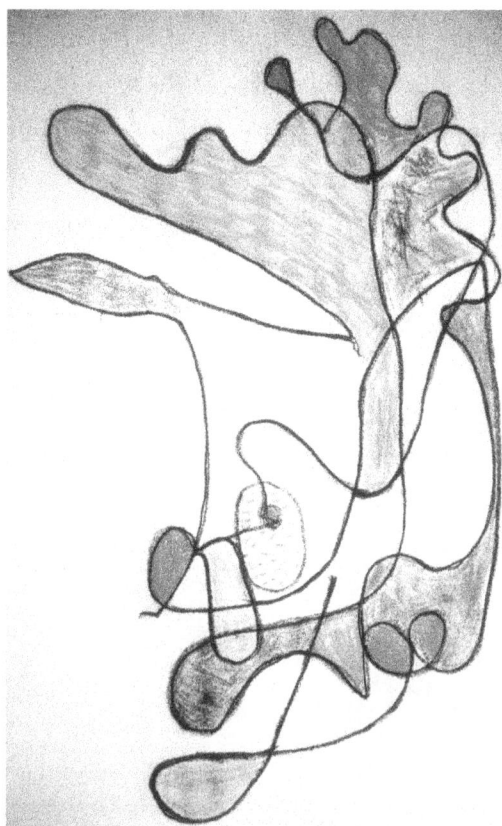

After Meditation - Coty Benrimoj

Before Meditation - Sam Fernandez

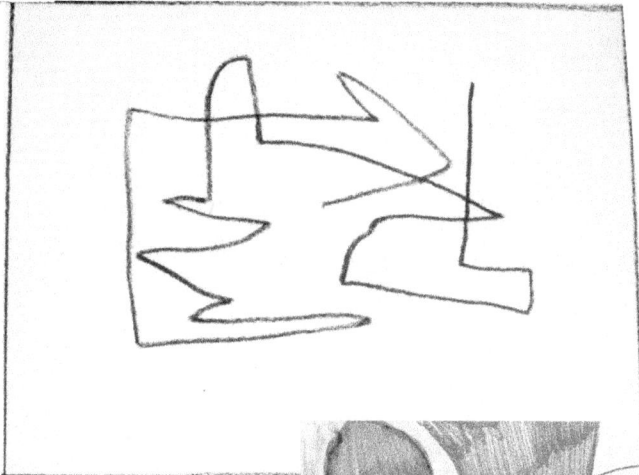

After Meditation
Sam Fernandez

"WHAT YOU ARE THE WORLD IS.
AND WITHOUT YOUR TRANSFORMATION
THERE CAN BE NO TRANSFORMATION
OF THE WORLD."
—J. KRISHNAMURTI

~ S e s s i o n 2 ~
TRANSFORMATION

Principle

Transformation.

Objective

The creative use of imagination.

Activity

Introduction, meditation and art project.

Materials

Soft pencils, markers or colored pencils.

An assortment of household tools, garden tools

or small carpentry tools.

INTRODUCTION

The concept of transformation addresses, among other issues, the question of power, personal and communal. In the face of problems, uncommon situations and circumstances, we often feel helpless and powerless to bring about changes. So it is essential that we learn to exercise the power of transformation, if for no other reason than to actually discover that we own this power within all of us. The "big one" is to consciously transform concepts of self-imposed limitations. But let us start with an exercise somewhat more modest and a lot more fun.

INTRODUCTIONS FOR ART ACTIVITY

Select one item from a group of objects provided. The group of objects can include tools such as kitchen utensils or small garden tools or such things as pliers, hammers, scissors, etc. Any interesting tools or utensils will do. On the upper left-hand corner of your drawing paper, make a simple, small drawing of your chosen object.

GUIDED MEDITATION

Close your eyes and deeply inhale and exale. While doing this, silently, in your mind, match your breathing with these words: inspiration, expiration, creation. Do this five times.

Now slowly open your eyes only half way so things appear slightly foggy. Stay in the meditative state. Pick up your selected object and contemplate it from all angles. Ask yourself, Does it have moving parts? Can it be viewed open or closed, upside down or sideways? We are now in an open eye meditation, viewing our object as we use our imagination to transform it from an inanimate object to something capable of motion. Simply ask yourself, If this thing were alive, what could it be? What could it do? What does it remind me of?

ART ACTIVITY

Here is an example: Look at a pair of scissors, open them and look again. What is it now? How about a creature running? Let your imagination run wild. In the upper left-hand corner, make a small drawing of the actual object. Use the entire paper to do a goodsize drawing of your chosen object transformed by your power to break through the illusion of limitation. You have much more power than you think to transform your environment and yourself within it. We will continue to exercise our power of transformation while we enjoy a great variety of art projects as a group. As artists, we can transform ourselves and the world around us.

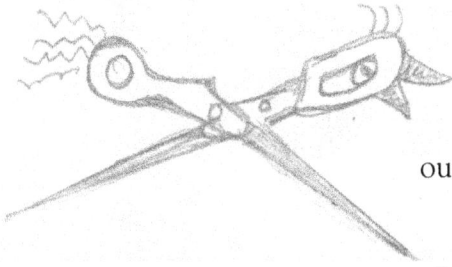

Do, share, discuss.

CLOSING MEDITATION

Close your eyes. Breathe deeply while you acknowledge the significant process you performed by transforming something ordinary into something you infused with your imagination. Contemplate the blessing of this power of transformation you possess. Inscribe it into your memory bank. (Remembering: when life hands you a lemon, make lemonade.) But honestly, nothing that comes into your life is against you, everything is for you. You have the power to transform the adverse into the advantageous or, with a sense of humor, you can transform the common place into the extraordinary.

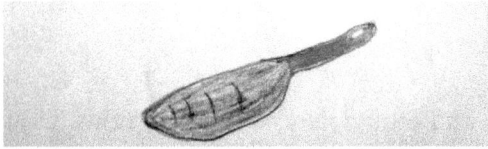

Before Transformation
Coty Benremoj

After Transformation
Coty Benremoj

Before Transformation - Pam Glover

After Transformation - Pam Glover

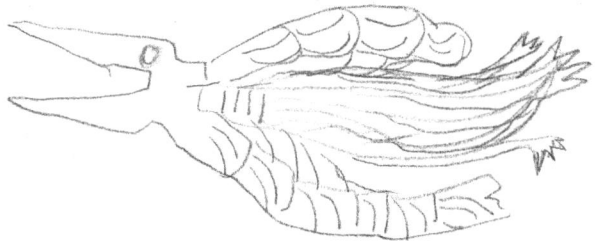

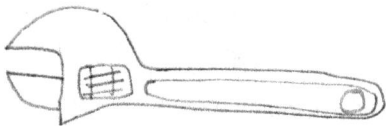

Before Transformation
Michael-Mhead Phillips

After Transformation
Michael-Mhead Phillips

Before Transformation - Rachel Forsyth

After Transformation - Rachel Forsyth

Before Transformation
Nancy Cohen-Dechter

After Transformation
Nancy Cohen-Dechter

TRANSFORMATION

Before Transformation
Nancy Cohen-Dechter

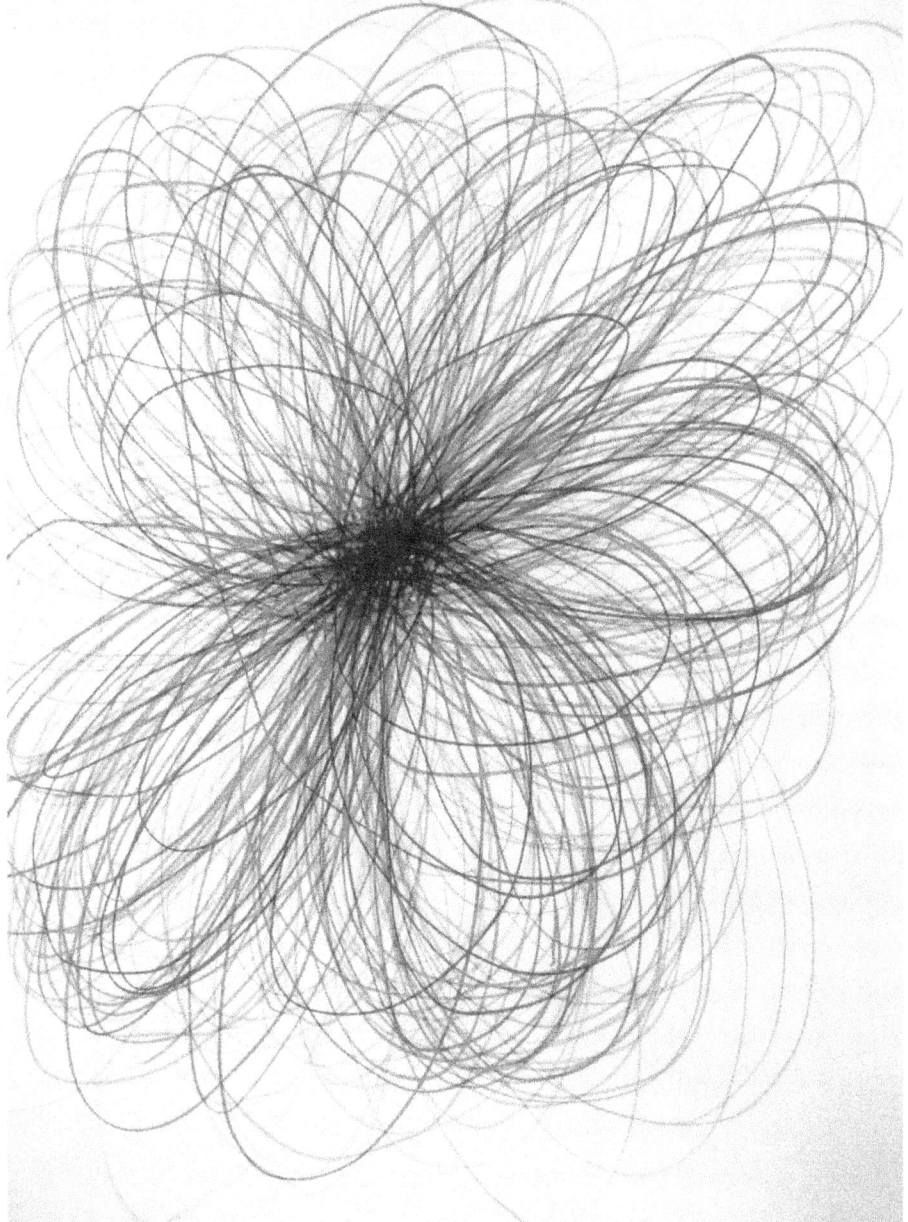

After Transformation
Nancy Cohen-Dechter

"LET'S TRADE IN ALL OUR JUDGING FOR APPRECIATING.
LET'S LAY DOWN OUR RIGHTEOUSNESS AND
JUST BE TOGETHER."
—Ram Dass

~ Session 3 ~
THE DIRECT EXPERIENCE

Principle
The direct experience.

Objective
Seeing without pre-judgment or interpretation.

Activities
Meditation and contour drawing without looking at the paper.

Materials
Soft pencils and drawing paper. A display of interesting-looking objects or subjects including fellow participants for portraits.

GUIDED MEDITATION

Close your eyes and take deep, even breathes. Detach yourself from the distraction of the environment, such as sounds and visual memories. Take your time to find your way to your creative inner core - the island of receptivity and undivided attention. Stay in this mode for several minutes.

ART ACTIVITY

Look at the objects provided for you to draw. Select one that interests you. You may want to pick it up, examine it and even run your fingers over its contours. Run your fingers over your object's outer contours as well as across its surface. Position yourself in front of the object and really see it. Look at it until you begin to sense a connection between you and your chosen object.

Now fix your eyes on a selected point anywhere on the contour of the object you will be drawing. Place the tip of the pencil on the corresponding spot on the paper. Do not start drawing until you get the sensation that your eyes and your pencil are touching the same spot on the object. Without looking at the paper, begin to draw very, very slowly, keeping the pencil on the paper at all times. Let your eyes move, following the contour of your object while the pencil follows to draw the same contour on the paper. Do not look at the paper. Keep the pencil moving ever so slowly without lifting it from the paper, around and across the form. Feel free to use the entire page for the drawing.

Do not worry about the accuracy and quality of your drawing. But maintain the sensation of your pencil being in direct contact with the object. Resist the temptation to look at the paper. If you should run off the paper just get back on. Reestablish the contact with the contour without taking your eyes off of your subject matter. Follow the lines and curves as they appear.

POST REFLECTION

This exercise is not about making a nice drawing. It is all about becoming one with the way you are feeling, seeing, doing and being. When we trust our direct experience, we are able to move beyond dependence on interpretation and judgment by the conditioned mind. Behold what you have created.

Suggested Practice: Listening without prejudgment or interpretation. Practice listening to others without judgments.

CLOSING MEDITATION

Close your eyes. Breathe deeply. *Silently repeat these thoughts:*

1. On the in breathe: I see . . .
On the out breath: Without pre-conceived judgments.

2. In: I release my expectations of . . .
Out: How things should look, act, feel, be.

3. In: I listen silently . . .
Out: Without forming a premature answer.

4. In: I observe . . .
Out: I acknowledge.

Open your eyes and look at each other as if for the first time. . .

Direct Experience
Esther Platner

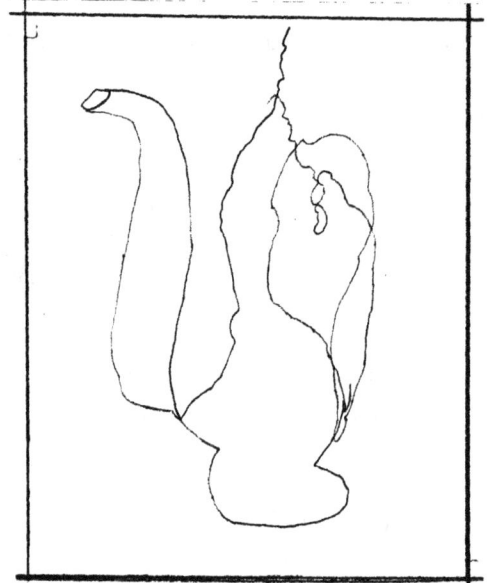

Direct Experience
Joel Paola

Direct Experience
Tyler Callison

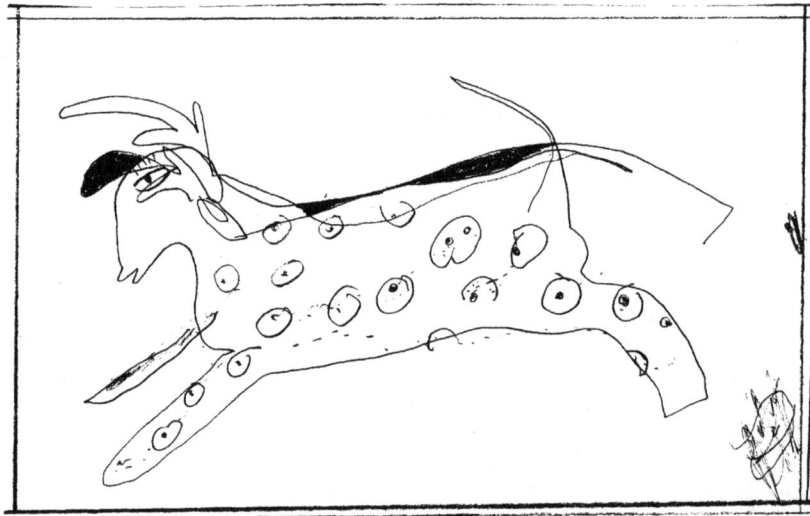

Direct Experience
Ron C. Dechter

Direct Experience
Nancy Cohen-Dechter

Direct Experience
Ron C. Dechter

Direct Experience
Joel Paola

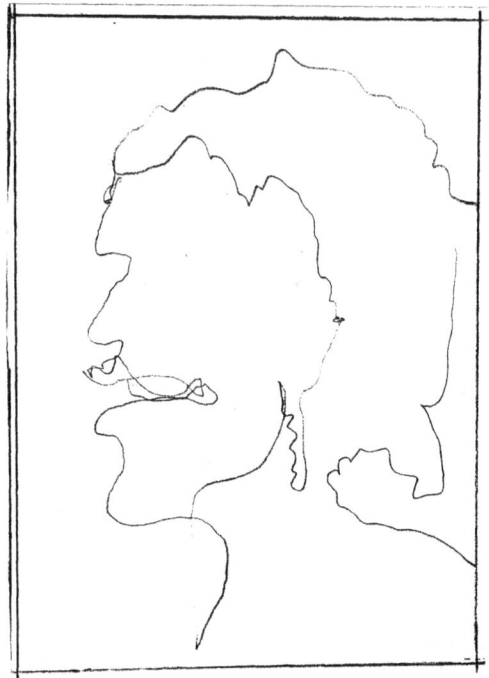

Direct Experience
Tyler Callison

Direct Experience
Esther Platner

~ NOTES ~

"LIBERTY AND UNION, NOW AND FOREVER,
ONE AND INSEPARABLE."
—Daniel Webster

~ Session 4 ~
THE INDIVIDUAL IN COMMUNITY

Principle
Individuality in community.

Objective
Losing the illusion of separateness.

Activity
Guided meditation and two art activities.

Materials
Fold a sheet of aluminum foil around a cardboard backing about 6 X 8" for each participant. Water-soluble colored markers. Spray bottle filled with 3 parts of water to 1 part of acrylic gloss medium. Part II: paper and soft pencils.

GUIDED MEDITATION

Take five deep breaths, imagine fresh snow on the ground. Make a snowball, nice, round and firm. Toss it into the ocean. Watch the snowball melt into the salty water. Picture the interaction between the individual units of sweet, frozen water in the vast, salty ocean. Observe and breath-slowly and deeply.

ART ACTIVITY 1

Select one color from a set of washable magic markers. Draw three free-form shapes using the markers, generously anywhere on the sheet of aluminum foil. Leave enough space for three more participants to do the same, each in a different color. Pass the sheet to the person next to you and repeat. It is okay for participants' shapes to touch one another. We will spray the finished picture with water and acrylic medium and watch the individual colors and shapes running together changing the separate contributions into one communal creation.

ART ACTIVITY 2

While the first project is drying, do this second activity: Use one pencil each and one sheet of paper for three participants. One person starts on top of the paper, drawing a head of a person or an animal, including the neck. Keep the drawing concealed. Fold the paper so that only a small piece is visible—just enough for the next person to know where to connect and continue the drawing of the body. The process continues through the third person, who draws the legs and feet. Unfold the paper and unveil what you have created together as a group of individuals in community!

CLOSING MEDITATION

With closed eyes, scan your body, head to toes, and back up to your head. Stay there and slow your breathing. For a moment, feel your existence as a complete and separate unit. Now listen to the breathing and feel the energy of all the "others" sharing this space with you. You can't help but drop the illusion of separateness. The "I" has become a "We." You are an integral unit within the totality of Being. Now begin to cultivate the awareness of your contribution as an individual to the collective consciousness. Feel the comfort and warmth of interbeing.

In a playful way, you have communicated the amazing effects of co-operation by creating together surprising pieces of art. You demonstrated the power of collective consciousness. You are never separate. Open your eyes and look deeply into the eyes of your communal co-creators.

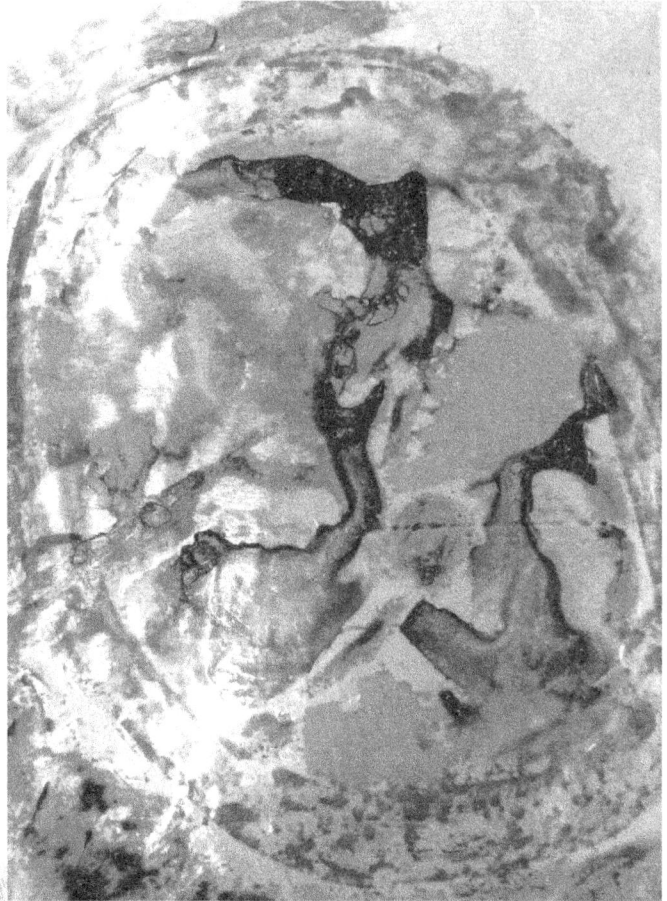

*Individual in Community
Group*

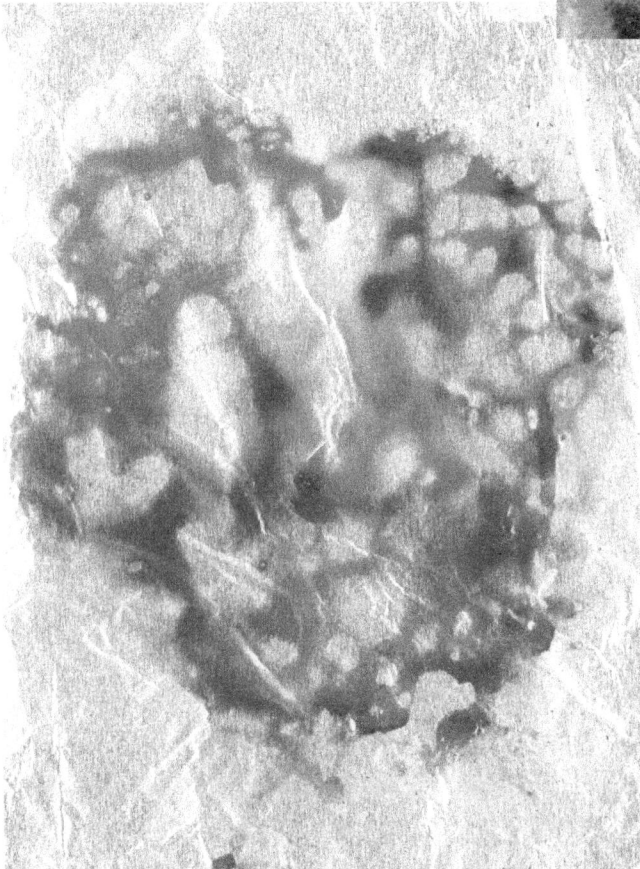

*Individual in Community
Group*

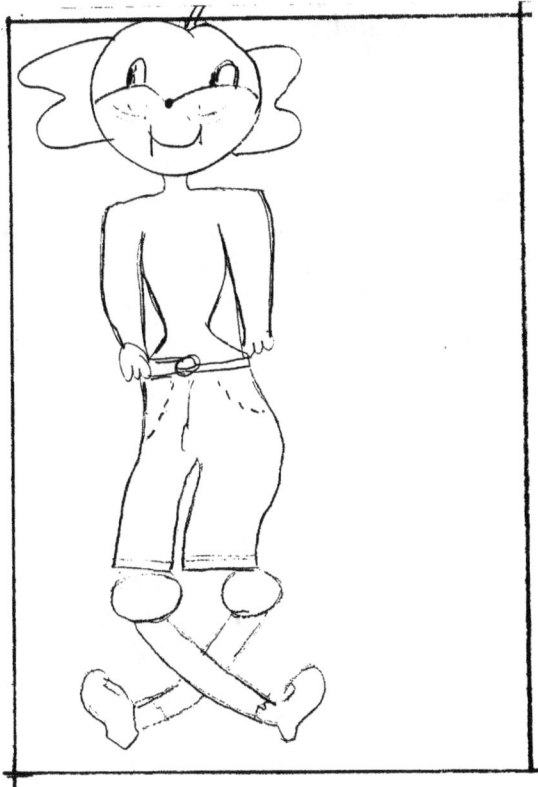

Individual in Community - Group

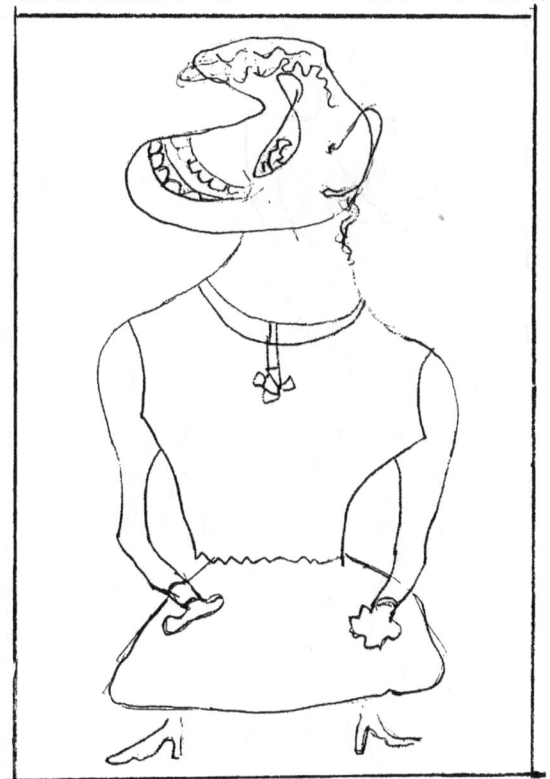

Individual in Community - Group

Individual in Community
Group

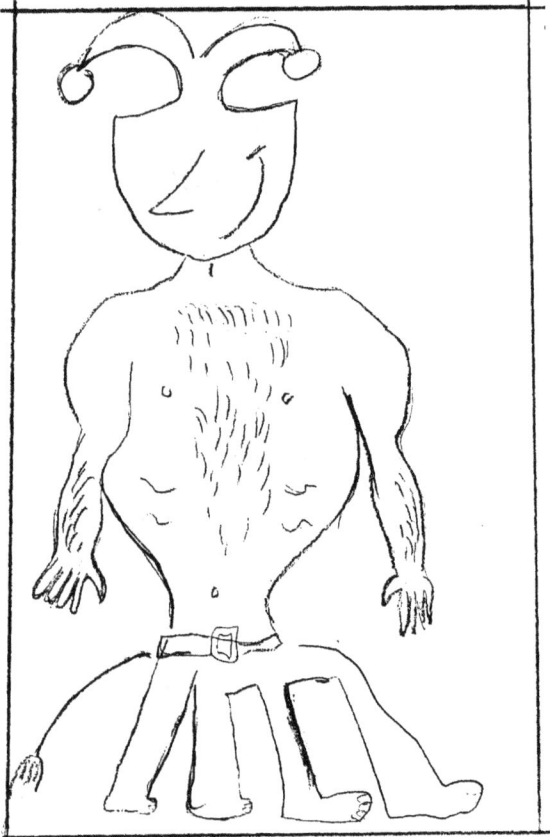

*Individual in Community
Group*

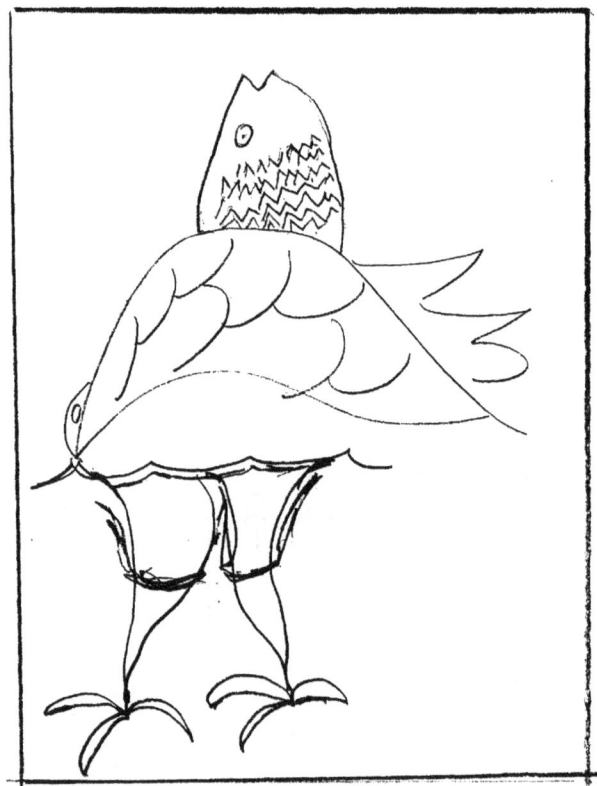

*Individual in Community
Group*

~ NOTES ~

"OUR SEPARATION OF EACH OTHER IS AN
OPTICAL ILLUSION OF CONSCIOUSNESS."
—Albert Einstein

~Session 5~
EVOLUTION—PERSONAL AND UNIVERSAL

Principle

Evolution—personal and universal.

Objective

Probing life as an ongoing process.

Activity

Guided meditation and drawing.

Materials

3 sheets of drawing paper per person. Soft pencils, crayons and colored markers.

INTRODUCTION

Evolution is a fascinating phenomenon that we more or less passively observe as it unfolds from the past. We also speculate about it as it concerns the future. The time has come when we need to go beyond eagerly confirming that it is indeed an ongoing process. Life is not a monologue. The next logical step is to awaken the awareness of the self within the totality of the evolutionary process. According to Rabbi Samuel Penner in *The four dimensions of paradise*, "Life is a creative dialogue to share so we can learn to fulfill those divine latencies resident within us, individually and socially." Thus, we become able to consciously partner with the concept of evolution.

MEDITATION

Close your eyes and take five deep breaths, inhale and exhale. You have evolved from an embryo and you have emerged into this world. You are totally dependent. All that supports you comes from those in your environment from the outside—in, physically and emotionality. You are loved and nurtured by those around you. Breathe into that feeling. Now move on to picture yourself as a two and half year old child. Gradually, important things and people in your world are taking on form and color.

ART ACTIVITY

Open your eyes and draw for three minutes. You are given your first crayon and paper to use. Be that two and half year old child and have your first experience with making marks on paper.

MEDITATION

Close your eyes again and take five deep breaths. You are growing and evolving into the consciousness of a five year old. You are encouraged in your learning process with loving feedback. Mommy shows you how to draw stick people and animals. You have favorite places, friends, toys—your world is expanding.

ART ACTIVITY

Open your eyes and draw for five minutes, make your best five year old drawing. You are making it all by yourself. How does it make you feel?

MEDITATION

Now close your eyes again. Take five deep breaths. Fast forward to your teenage years, remember how all along you have been motivated mostly by those in the world, which supports you and molds you from the outside in. But what do you do about that new inner voice that is often not in harmony with your support system? Will it have to wait until your survival is no longer dependent only on the support and approval from the outside world alone? Feel all that arises within the process… How would it feel to express what concerned you at this stage of your evolution? Feel all that arises within you.

ART ACTIVITY

Now open your eyes. Express the memory of your personal evolution in a drawing. Include all that arises from the memories of your teenage years when you have experienced the passage from total dependency and outer-direction to the challenges of exploring inner-direction.

MEDITATION

Close your eyes, take deep breaths. Be you now. Feel how you have gradually found refuge within yourself. Accept whatever you have found in this inner space to work with. You have evolved from being outer—directed to being inner—directed. Dwell in this space for a while.

SUMMARY

Your inner world contains the seeds for your personal ongoing evolution. It is the reservoir containing your creativity. Let us give some thoughts to the ways in which our awakened awareness can help us to meet the challenges presented by life, not only personal but also universal. How can we consciously participate in the process of evolution in a constructive way? Here are some suggestions for a mantra:

1. I am expanding my observation of cause and effect.
2. I am being consciously selective about the sources guiding my choices and decisions.
3. I am intending my actions to promote the most beneficial impact upon our world and the individuals within it.

Let us continue the fun with a homework project: revisit your inner child and create an art piece in which you, the evolved adult, allow the child in you to freely express itself. It can be a drawing, a painting, a collage, a poem or story, anything that calls to you from the inside.

CLOSING MEDITATION

Breathe deeply and evenly. Confirm with your whole Being the blessings of the ongoing processes in life. We are never "finished," as long as we observe the unfolding of the messages and directions coming to us from our center. Promise yourself to trust your inner guidance in the process of continuing evolution. You have progressed from being outer-directed to being inner-directed. Open your eyes and feel the blessings in and around you.

Evolution - 2½ year old

*Evolution
5 year old*

Evolution
5 year old

Evolution - Young adult

Evolution - Teen years

Evolution - Teen years

"ROUGH DIAMONDS MAY SOMETIMES BE
MISTAKEN FOR WORTHLESS PEBBLES."
—Sir Thomas Brown

~Session 6~
RECOGNIZING POTENTIAL

Principle

Recognizing potential.

Objective

Connecting with the elements of nature.

Activity

Meditation and creating a pendent necklace.

Materials

Colored glass pebbles or interesting stones, soft jewelry wire, jewelry pliers, cord.

INTRODUCTION

You will create a necklace (if you want to!). This piece of jewelry can be worn to connect the wearer with nature's elemental energy. Colored glass pebbles will be wrapped with wire. These are simple items that we accept and use without giving much thought to their origin. At this time, let us contemplate the process by which molten sand becomes glass and ore was spun into a thread of metal, wire.

MEDITATION

Choose your pebble and hold it in your hand. With eyes closed, take five deep breaths, inhale and exhale. Contemplate the heat of fire that was the catalyst for transformation. The element of nature, fire is essential to life and transformation. Breathe deeply five times. Imagine sitting around a blazing camp fire with the members of your clan. There is chanting and storytelling going on. You feel the energy of the community. Together you feel the energy of the fire, primal and essential for survival, purification and evolution. Transpose these powerful images into the simple things we do and use in everyday life and that we take for granted. They carry energy derived from the interaction between the elements of nature. When we recognize the inherent potential, we can transform the overtly common place with our creative energy.

ART ACTIVITY

Surround and embellish the glass bead with a wire wrapping. Take your time and enjoy the awareness that the metal in the wire has electrical energy. It conducts and increases the energy to raise the vibrations. View some examples for inspiration.

MEDITATION

Take five deep breaths, inhale and exhale. Hold your finished piece in your closed hand. Join your own vibrational energy with that of your creation. What is its potential in connecting you to the elements of nature?

You can infuse your creation with the energies of your personal vision.

Open your eyes. Finish your pendant with a chord to be worn around your neck. Wear it and feel it.

CLOSING MEDITATION

Once more, close your eyes for a few moments. Allow yourself to feel your consciousness expanding from now to the future—where you can't avoid noticing the transformational possibilities all around you, including anything found in nature or trash. Your life can actually become an Art Process.

Open your eyes and feel related with a sense of "allowing."

Realizing Potential - Sandee Ruckersberg and Ruth Platner

~ NOTES ~

"EVERYTHING FLOWS AND NOTHING ABIDES,
EVERYTHING GIVES WAY AND
NOTHING STAYS FIXED."
—Heraclitus

~ Session 7 ~
IMPERMANENCE AND DETACHMENT

Principle

Impermanence and detachment.

Objective

Get over it!

Activity

Meditation, sculpting with clay and discussion.

Materials

Air dry modeling clay and a firm surface to work on.

GUIDED MEDITATION

Breathe deeply, picture yourself in the center of a glorious field of flowers. Inhale the scents. You experience the colors and intricate shapes and the intoxicating fragrance that surrounds you. Your spirits are elevated. You would like this experience to last forever. Suddenly, the flowers start to wilt and die. You observe the process helplessly. The loss of all the loveliness is so sad. You want to get past the pain of loss—past the attachment to your experience in the midst of this perfect beauty. Sadly, you focus downward on the decaying flowers. As you behold impermanence, you become aware of the dark, fertile soil beneath. Slowly you begin to realize that new fresh flowers will grow fertilized by the dead ones. You can now let go, practicing detachment, realizing that in the face of impermanence, detachment equals trust in the ongoing process of evolution.

ART ACTIVITY

The participants receive two lumps of clay, the size of a golf ball each, to make two sculptures of their choice. Example: small animals or human head, etc. Take about 15 minutes to make the objects. Put both pieces on a firm surface. Put one hand over the sculpture of your choice. With your other hand, smash it.

DISCUSSION

What now? How do I feel? What can I do?

OPTIONS

Fix the smashed sculpture or make a new one or you could practice detachment once more by giving away the intact sculpture. Give and receive!

CLOSING MEDITATION

Close your eyes and listen to your breath for a few moments. Allow yourself to become very calm.

Inhale silently saying: "Full"

Exhale silently saying: "Empty"

Inhale silently saying: "Receiving"

Exhale silently saying: "Giving"

Inhale silently saying: "Holding"

Exhale silently saying: "Letting Go"

Inhale and exhale saying: "Loss"

Inhale and exhale saying: "Regeneration"

Impermanence and detachment - Sam Fernandez

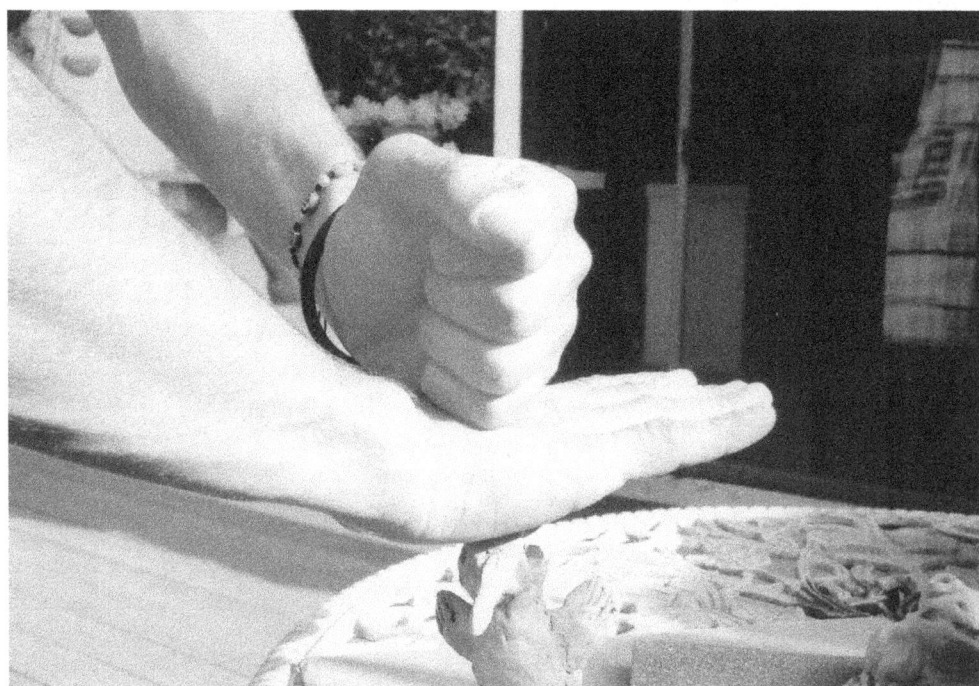

Impermanence and detachment - Sam Fernandez

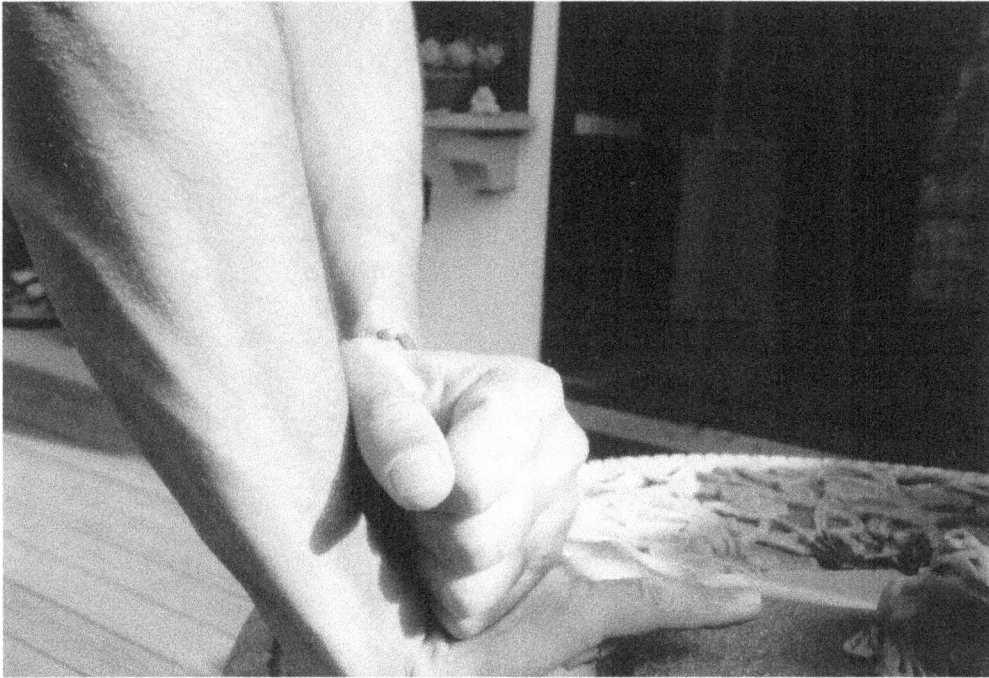

Impermanence and detachment - Sam Fernandez

Impermanence and detachment - Sam Fernandez

"THERE'S NO SECRET TO BALANCE.
YOU JUST HAVE TO FEEL THE WAVES."
— FRANK HERBERT

~ Session 8 ~
FOUNDATION, STRUCTURE & BALANCE

Principle

Foundation, structure and balance.

Objective

From trash to art.

Materials

Empty cereal boxes or cartons of any kind, scissors and tape.

INTRODUCTION TO ART ACTIVITY

Create a freestanding sculpture from the cardboard provided. We will start by constructing a foundation upon which to build and balance a structure. Select several pieces of cardboard for the base and body of your sculpture.

GUIDED MEDITATION

Take deep breaths, inhale, and exhale, balance your inhale with your exhale. Contemplate that fact that everything in the physical world has structure that is supported by a foundation, and balance keeps the structure from collapsing. Just sit with this for a few minutes and imagine yourself attempting to erect a freestanding structure using these principles.

For about five minutes, breathe deeply while repeating silently the words "Foundation, Structure, Balance."

ART ACTIVITY

Examine the sample provided. Select pieces of cardboard which appear to be suitable for the construction of a foundation. Cut one- to two-inch slits into the cardboard so that you can connect the pieces together. The foundation can be a rectangle, U shape, triangle or round. The important thing is to create a sturdy base to support the structure you are building. The structural components are created by cutting out interesting shapes in various sizes from the cardboard. These pieces are fitted to each other by cutting one-inch slits where they connect. It will become evident now how essential balance is when we are creating anything. The sculptural structure is developed by adding and connecting shapes to one another. With proper attention to balance, the sculpture can be built up to the desired height. Balance is achieved by connecting pieces to each other, pointing in various opposing directions. The structure can be supported with tape if needed.

Behold! Potential trash has been transformed by you into art. Think about foundation, structure and balance in your life and life in general.

CLOSING MEDITATION

With closed eyes, breathe deeply into the recall of the beautiful sculpture you have created from simple, actually throw-away materials. You have metaphorically demonstrated the universal principle of manifestation in the world of duality. Here, everything we do, everything we bring into existence, has to have structure, supported and resting upon a foundation.

Now, connect deeply into your center of consciousness and, here, plant and cultivate the ultimate creative principle: Balance. Let us consider balance in all our "doings."

Structure and Balance
Sam Fernandez

Structure and Balance
Michael-Mhead Phillips

Structure and Balance
Ruth Platner

Structure and Balance
Ron C. Dechter

"THE PURE IMPULSE OF DYNAMIC CREATION IS FORMLESS;
AND BEING FORMLESS, THE CREATION IT GIVES RISE
TO CAN ASSUME ANY AND EVERY FORM."
—THE KABBALAH

~ Session 9 ~
FORM AND THE FORMLESS

Principle

Form and the formless.

Objective

To feel supported.

Materials

EXERCISE 1

Pictures from magazines showing a figure or object in the foreground.

EXERCISE 2

A 4 X 8 piece of art paper that has been textured and a soft
pencil for each participant.

INTRODUCTION

Human beings cannot mentally know what lies beyond human form. Formless space is conceived as the background for the manifest form, with the human form considered to be the most evolved and blessed with the highest consciousness.

In art terms, the space surrounding the forms depicted in a painting or a drawing is called a "negative space." This is not meant to be a value judgment. Negative space appears to be altered by the placement and movement of manifest form within it. This idea deserves reconsideration, as it is an illusion resulting from the superior importance we as human beings assign to form over formlessness.

An exercise will help us reexamine the relationship between the form and the formless.

ART EXERCISE 1

Given a picture showing objects or figures in a surrounding, draw a strong visible line around negative space areas. Shade or color inside of all negative space areas, all in the same color or shade.

<u>You will make the important discovery that the so-called negative space, which is in essence formless, in actuality defines and even supports the forms within its realm.</u>

MEDITATION

Close your eyes. Take five breaths. Allow your formed thoughts to become weightless in formless space. Feel yourself in perfect harmony with everything. Observe your form floating and supported by non-duality. Open yourself to being changed by ever-new insights coming to you out of formless space to be made manifest here and now. When we are in the process of creating art, we become conscious participants in the interaction between form and the formless, which is also known as the spirit.

ART EXERCISE 2

Use a sheet of paper that has been given a subtle textured pattern.* Contemplate this essentially formless space. Allow your imagination to discover and create a form or forms revealed to you within this formless space. Define what you see, using a pencil.

Share and discuss what you have created.

CLOSING MEDITATION

In this meditation, let us practice the old art of CLOUD READING. Behind closed eyes, picture yourself flat on your back in a meadow. In the sky, cloud formations float by. Interesting forms come and go. We see faces, animals, etc. All these are projections from our inner screen, coming and going. However, the formless background of space remains the same. We may ponder what it is that defines us. How much of what we believe we are comes from the interaction with other life-forms, like family, society and/or culture? What in us seems to originate from formless space or spirit? I would suggest that it is not "This or that," but it is "This and that".

*I use a small sponge to stipple a layer of yellow paint onto the paper, followed by a layer of stippling with a slightly darker shade. (I used yellow ochre).

Form and the Formless - Ruth Platner

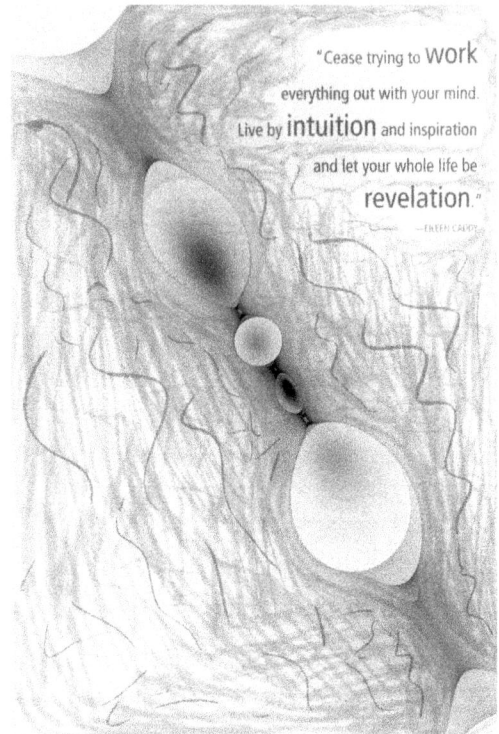

"Cease trying to work everything out with your mind. Live by intuition and inspiration and let your whole life be revelation."

—EILEEN CADDY

Form and the Formless - Elena Zone

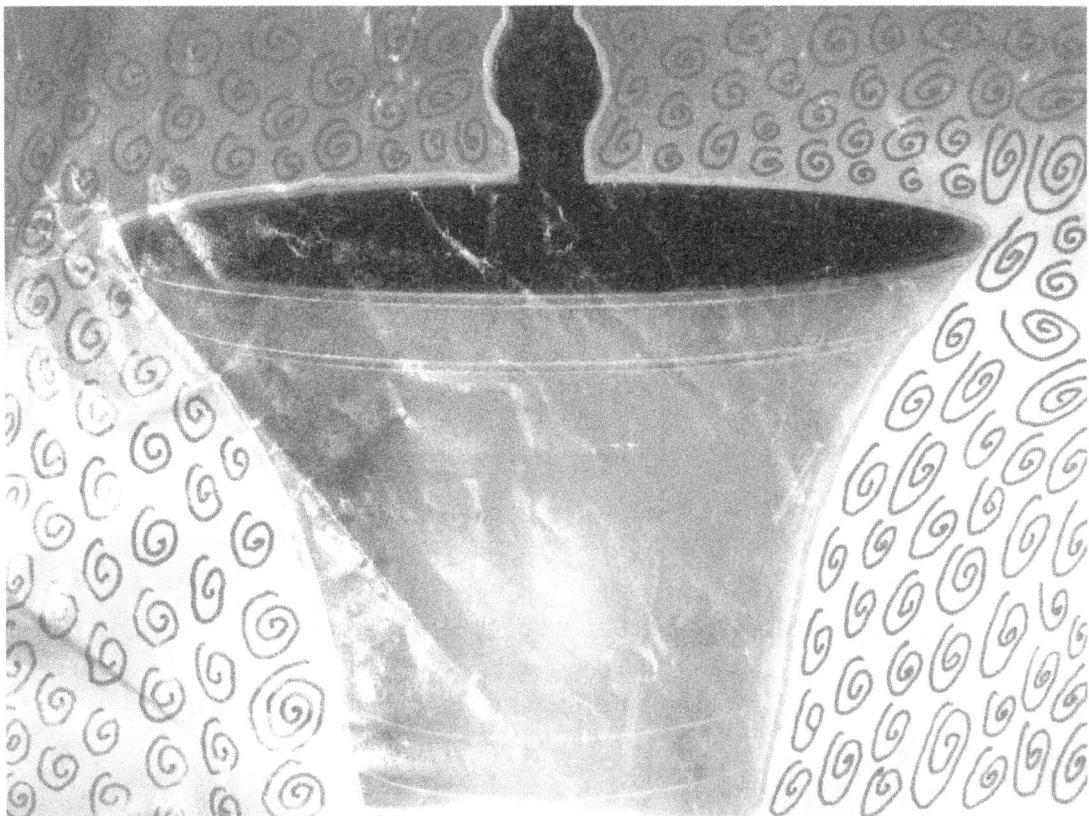

Form and the Formless - Ron C. Dechter

Form and the Formless

Form and the Formless

Form and the Formless

MEDITATION & ART

HANDOUT FOR SESSION 10, TO BE DISTRIBUTED AFTER SESSION 9.

Principle
Celebrating gifts from nature.

Objective
Sticks and stones transformed to create a nature spirit doll.

Introduction
A nature walk cannot fail to reveal the treasures all around us. We admire the grandeur of trees, the delicate beauty of plants, the fragrance of flowers and we enjoy the land and seascapes in general. On our way, we pass and step on pieces of nature without much thought or even notice. There are so many dry sticks, stones and seed pods just lying around. But there is another way to experience. A new way of discovery that can be pursued. We can become sensitive to ignored unsung treasures all around us. These can become our inspiration for our creations: Making stick figures. Some of the materials can be provided. However, between now and the next session you can go on you own treasure hunt. Please collect the following materials . . .

Materials
Three sticks, about 12" long for the arms and legs of a doll. For the head, collect a stone or you can use cloth and stuff it to create a ball. For the body, bring an empty toilet paper tube. Find something that is suitable for hair such as dry seaweed, yarn or anything that inspires you. The body can be wrapped in bark from the eucalyptus tree or from a palm tree or a banana plant or even colored cloth. Be inventive in your scrounging for decorations. (Old jewelry, seed pods, shells, beads, etc.). Bring all the treasures that sparked your imagination. We will use a glue gun to connect the parts at our next meeting. If you own a glue gun, please bring it.

NOTE: Please make a copy for each participant.

"IN ALL THINGS OF NATURE THERE IS
SOMETHING OF THE MARVELOUS."
—ARISTOTLE

CELEBRATING GIFTS FROM NATURE

Principle

Celebrating gifts from nature.

Objective

Sticks and stones transformed to create a nature spirit doll.

Introduction

A nature walk cannot fail to reveal the treasures all around us. We admire the grandeur of trees, the delicate beauty of plants, the fragrance of flowers and we enjoy the land and seascapes in general. On our way, we pass and step on pieces of nature without much thought or even notice. There are so many dry sticks, stones and seed pods just lying around. But there is another way to experience. A new way of discovery that can be pursued. We can become sensitive to ignored unsung treasures all around us. These can become our inspiration for our creations: making stick figures. I like to call them nature spirits . . .

Materials

Three sticks, about 12" long for the arms and legs of a doll. For the head, collect a stone or you can use cloth and stuff it to create a ball. For the body, bring an empty toilet paper tube. Find something that is suitable for hair such as dry seaweed, yarn or anything that inspires you. The body can be wrapped in bark from the eucalyptus tree or from a palm tree or a banana plant or even colored cloth. Be inventive in your scrounging for decorations. (Old jewelry, seed pods, shells, beads, etc.). Bring all the treasures that sparked your imagination. We will use a glue gun to connect the parts.

NOTE: It is a good idea to have extra materials on hand for people who did not receive the handout after Session #9.

GUIDED MEDITATION

We will begin by renewing our contact with nature, which provided all the treasures for our project. Remember how you felt when you were collecting these items. See if you can connect to old tribal memories or make up a story about the transformation you are about to bring about with these collected items. Unleash your imagination about this story character you are about to create. Be still and accept what arises.

ART ACTIVITY

The assembly of the nature spirit doll will be demonstrated and assisted (see next page). Embellish your character to your heart's delight. When finished, take your character from nature creation into contemplation, holding it caringly with both hands.

CLOSING MEDITATION

With your eyes closed, take five deep breaths:
1. Silently declare your gratitude to nature for her gift to you. Take deep breaths—inhale and exhale.
2. Celebrate your personal creativity in transforming; i.e., shaping some seemingly insignificant bits of nature into your very individual expression of art. Take deep breaths.
3. Infuse your creation with your personal energy and power; give it a name as you consciously breathe five deep breaths into it.

ART ACTIVITY

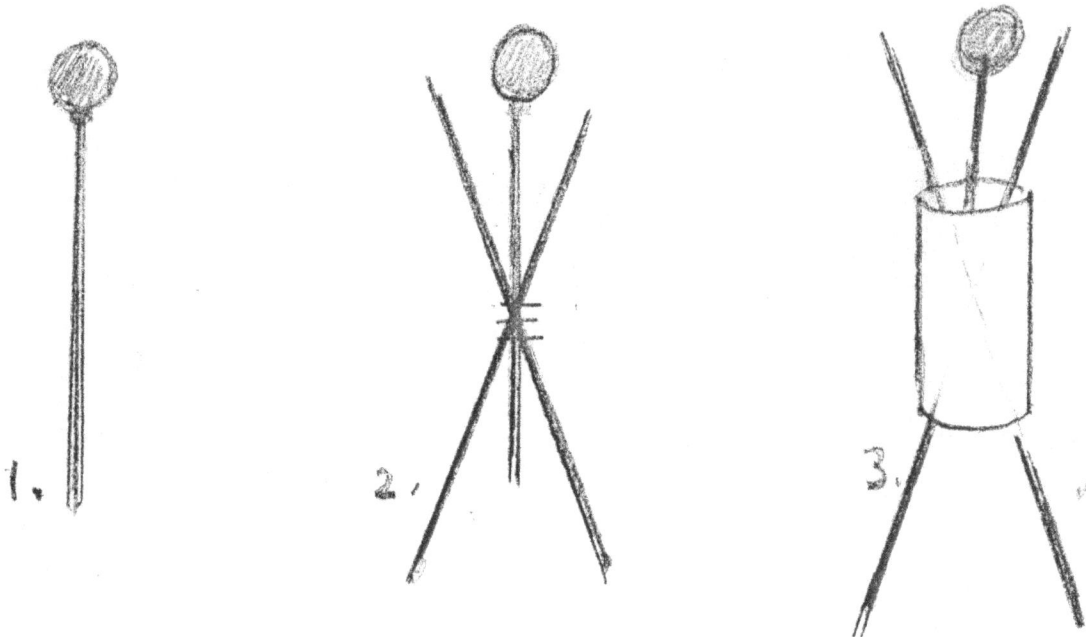

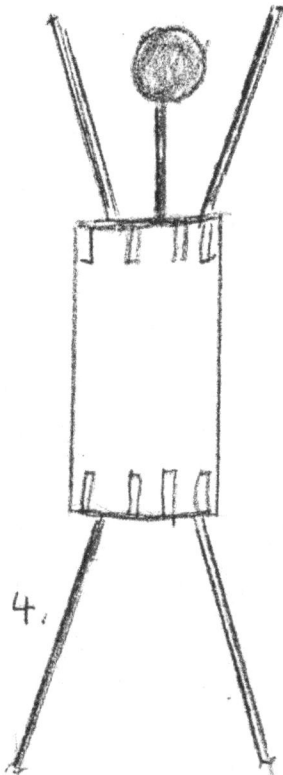

The Assembly of the Doll:

1. FASTEN the head to one stick.
2. BUNDLE three sticks and tie them together.
3. PUSH the sticks through the tube.
4. FLATTEN the tube and tape top and bottom areas to keep sticks in place.
5. DECORATE and embellish to your heart's content. →

Gifts from Nature - Jan Bayer

Gifts from Nature - Coty Benrimoj

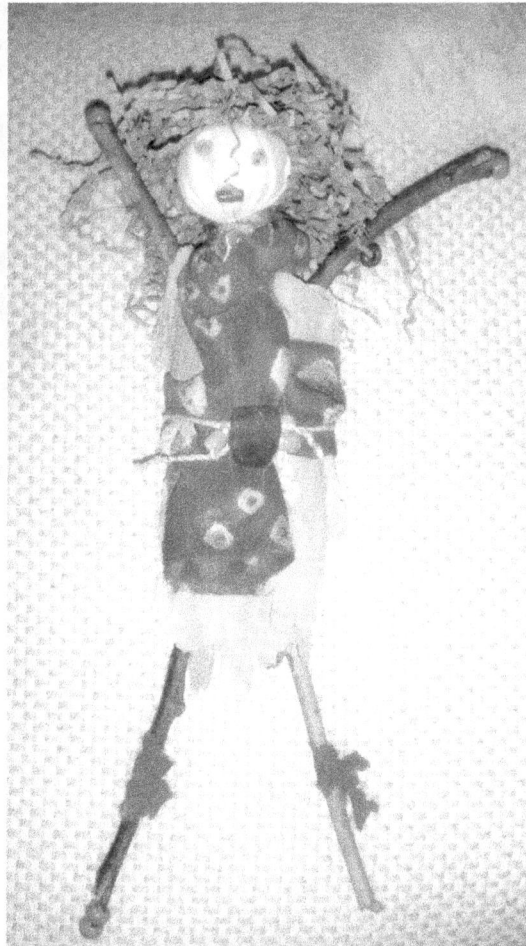

Gifts from Nature - Victor Sturm

Gifts from Nature - Ann Hunter

"RELATIVITY TEACHES US THE CONNECTION BETWEEN
THE DIFFERENT DESCRIPTIONS OF ONE
AND THE SAME REALITY."
— ALBERT EINSTEIN

~ Session 11 ~
RELATIVITY

Principle
Relativity.

Objective
Individuality vs. Conformity.

Materials
Paper, colored pencils or markers, a viewing frame,

two or more still lifes set up in the art activity space.

(Still life should not be too complex. See example.)

DISCUSSION

We see everything through our personal perspective. How do we develop this perspective? We seek to understand our personal experiences by interpreting them. We are looking for meaning, both personal and collective. Communicating personal perspective evolves along with our experiences. In organized society, there is usually a greater effort made in behalf of uniformity than for individuality. The truth remains that each of us will experience life from our personal perspective, which includes all we are and have been in our lifetimes and in our social experiences. Art is communication based on the artist's personal perspective of life and meaning. Viewers of art will interpret what they see based on their personal perspective.

QUESTION

If everything is relative, is there nothing absolute?

ANSWER

Absolutely not!

MEDITATION

Close your eyes breathe deeply and focus on absolutely nothing. Stay open to anything that arises.

ART ACTIVITY

Use colored pencils or markers to express yourself freely. Start by choosing any subject matter which interests you enough to communicate your personal perspective. You can make use of the provided still lifes or any object you see. The essential tool for this exercise is the viewing frame (provided). This tool will help you to decide what your personal perspective concerning the subject matter of your choice is going to include. Experiment with holding the viewing frame close to your eyes. You will see the entire panorama before you. Next, move the frame gradually away from your eyes, you will view a continuously smaller portion. For example, when your subject matter is a still life, as set up for this exercise, you can now choose your personal perspective, or viewpoint, to decide which part of the still life you want to include in your painting or drawing. You can also focus your attention on a very small portion or a detail which interests you by holding the frame far from your face, close to the subject matter. When you do your artwork, you always have the freedom to express your personal perspective—your very own point of view! To decide what that is, consult your feelings and bravely go with whatever arises, may it come from your intellect, your past or your fantasy.

CLOSING MEDITATION

Let us close our eyes and ears to external stimuli for a while. With each breath move a little deeper into inner space. What you see there will determine your priorities. These will shape your personal perspective of the world. Your perspective is instrumental in your approach to life. You have the choice always to express a variety of your viewpoints from different perspectives—ranging from the most inclusive to the most focused on detail. Cherish the fountain of inner knowledge.

*Examples of
objects seen
through the
viewing frame
from various
distances.*

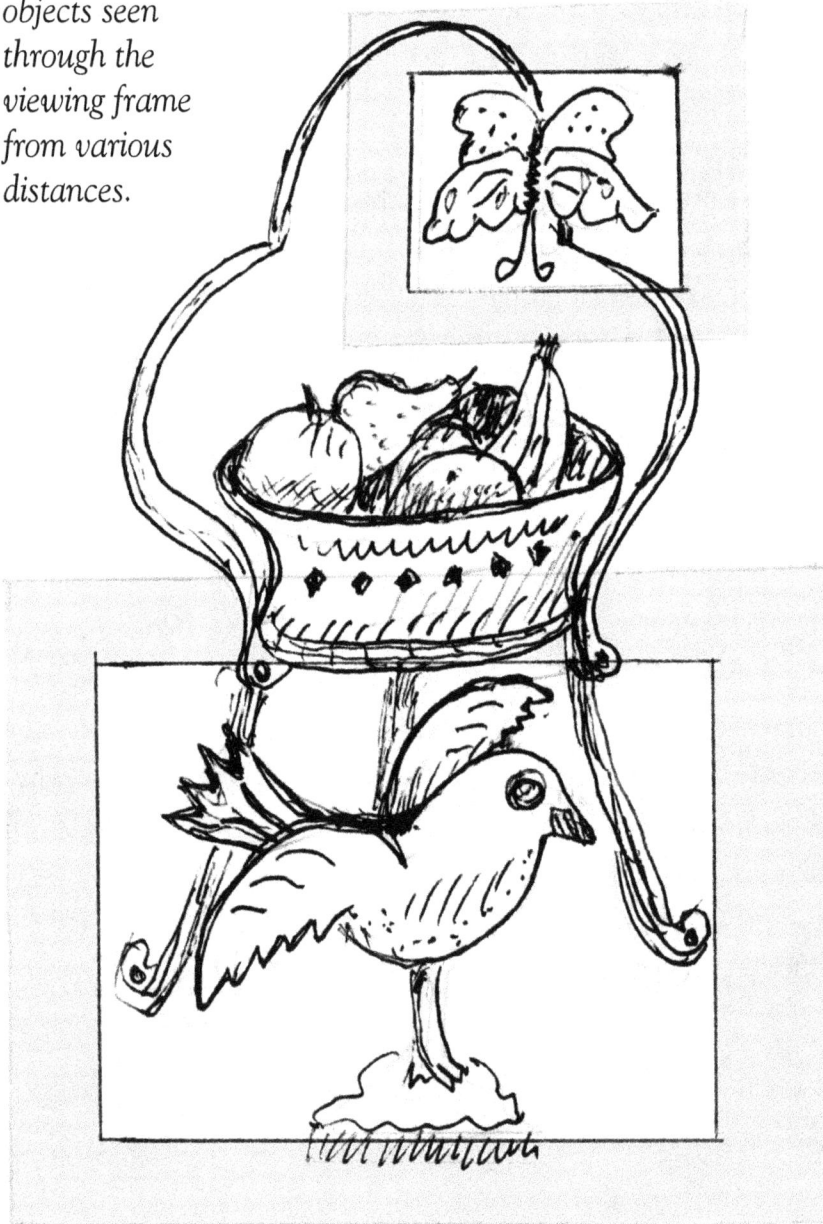

Relativity - Michael-Mhead Phillips

Relativity - Kambiz Jahan Giri

Relativity - Victor Sturm

Relativity
Nancy Cohen-
Dechter

Relativity
Sandee Ruckersberg

Relativity
Coty Benrimoj

"IT IS THROUGH COOPERATION,
RATHER THAN CONFLICT,
THAT YOUR GREATEST SUCCESSES
WILL BE DERIVED."
—RALPH CHARELL

~ S e s s i o n 12 ~
COOPERATION VS. COMPETITION

Principle

Cooperation vs. competition.

Objective

Mandalas for peace, created with group energy.

Materials

Paper with a large circle drawn on it. Soft pencil.

Drafting tools such as rulers, circles, templates, etc.

NARRATIVE

It takes practice to free ourselves from such concepts as "competition drives progress." That works for those who see life as a quantitative process, but competition is not the essence for a mainly qualitative point of view.

Competition locks us into a polarized worldview, where we strive for more, faster, stronger, better than, etc… All this binds us to the illusion of separateness: we must have a competitor to keep this process going or even more efficient—an enemy. Even a nation under the illusion of superiority will claim that it is destined to rule and control other nations. Much like corporate competition, conflicts are usually bitter and without any cooperative resolution in sight. This has no value in terms of evolving consciousness, which is so desperately needed to sustain life on earth along with growing quality for all.

Cooperation takes conscious practice, since it is not driven by lower instincts for dominance, which made some sense in primitive times. Let us fast-forward to the higher consciousness we have learned to appreciate within ourselves and in others.

MEDITATION

With closed eyes, feel the presence of all in this group. Together we will create sacred circles known as mandalas. Breath deeply while contemplating the joy of cooperating creatively. Deeply feel the peaceful sensation of creating together.

ART ACTIVITY

Given a sheet of paper with a large circle already drawn, divide the circle into sections and then hand the sheet to the person next to you. Continue by further dividing and or drawing designs into the sections. Keep moving the sheets around until you see the mandalas are complete. You will enhance each other's experience.

OPEN-EYE MEDITATION

View the mandala before you. Contemplate the concepts and results of cooperation and peace. Compose a message based on these concepts to accompany the mandala you are holding. We will make a coloring book from this collection, which you can duplicate and give to others as a gift of beautiful peaceful cooperation if you please.

CLOSING MEDITATION

With closed eyes, take several deep, soothing breaths. One by one, let us recall the universal principles we have acknowledged and internalized during meditations. Repeat after me silently:

1. Awareness.
2. Transformation.
3. Direct experience.
4. Individuality and community.
5. Evolution
6. Recognizing potential.
7. Impermanence and detachment.
8. Foundation, structure & balance.
9. Form and the formless.
10. Celebrating gifts from nature.
11. Relativity.
12. Cooperation vs. competition.

Together, you have created artworks, manifesting insights. These realizations are of great value to everyone of us in the process of conducting our daily life in community. Visualize yourself sharing your wisdom with others in your world.

CAUTION: Cooperation may cause peace.

AFFIRMATIONS BY
MICHAEL-MHEAD PHILLIPS

1. I am manifesting my inner visions and desires, using meditation as the creative art inspiration.

2. With my hands and heart, I am making my dreams real.

3. I am being a creator of beautiful thoughts, ideas and things.

4. I am a creative individual who knows how to make dreams real.

5. My imagination is boundless and my ideas flow like water.

6. I make something beautiful out of thin air.

7. I am using meditation to manifest art.

8. My mind and brain are elastic like a rubber band and the more I stretch, the more flexible I become.

Please feel free to add your own affirmations.

COOPERATIVE

MANDALA
COLORING BOOK

MICHAEL-MHEAD PHILLIPS

sandee rockenberg

VICTOR STURM

Jennifer Walker

Coty Benning

Maggie Clark

Therese-George-Harvey

Richard L Davidson

Elena Zone

THESE PEOPLE COOPERATED
TO CREATE THE MANDALAS
AND THE MESSAGES.

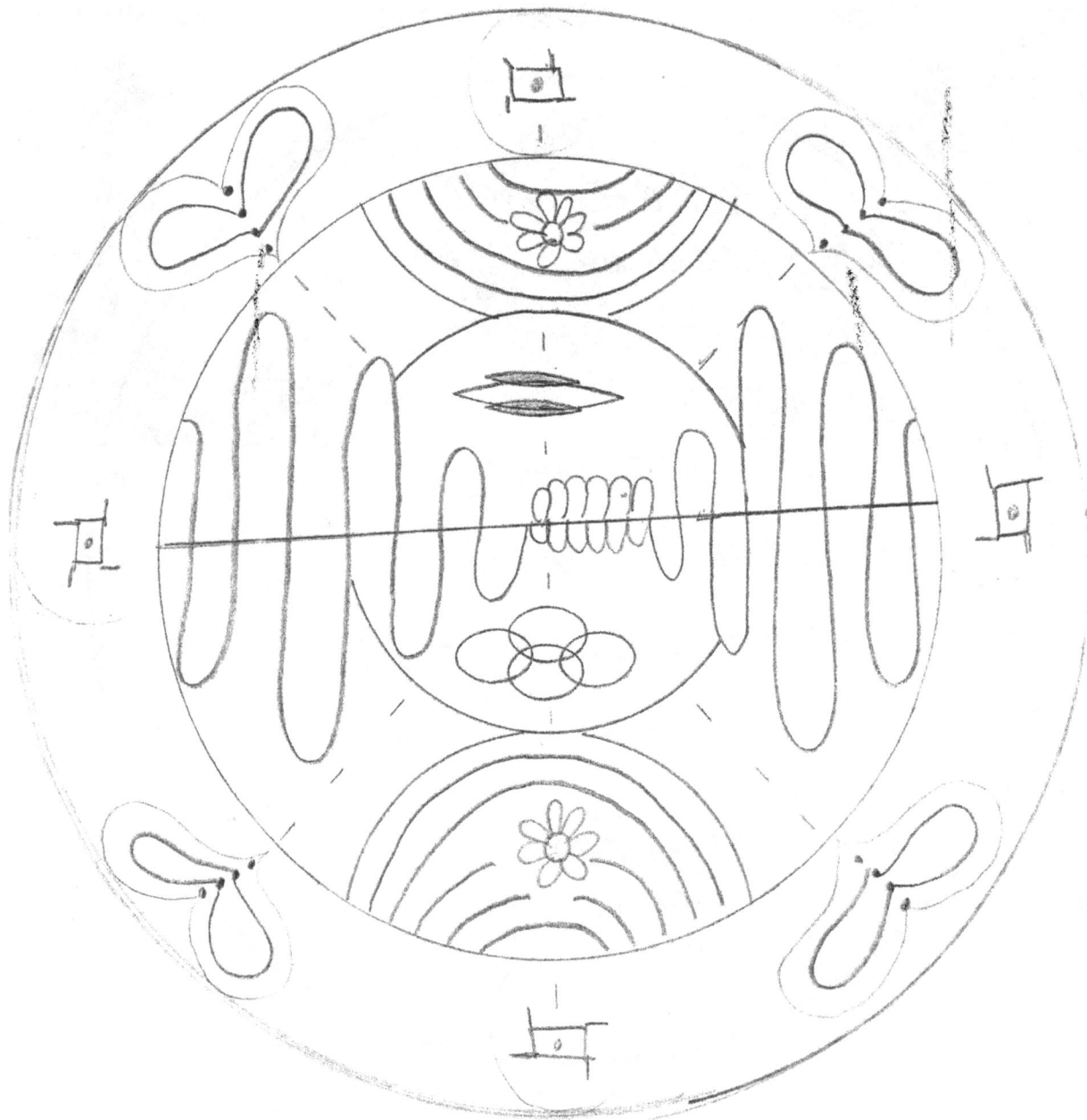

PEACE AND HARMONY ARE RESONANT
NOTES IN A SOMETIMES DISSONANT
SONG, ALWAYS COMPLIMENTING
THE WHOLE.

COOPERATION IS UNDIVIDED
ATTENTION THAT BRINGS
JOY AND HARMONY.

VISUALIZE THE BEST POSSIBLE
OUTCOME AND ACT AS IF IT HAS
ALREADY BEEN ACHIEVED.

Believe in Peace and Love and
the Oneness of all humanity.

FREEDOM, HOPE, LAUGHTER,
HARMONY = LOVE, THE
ENDLESS POTENTIAL.

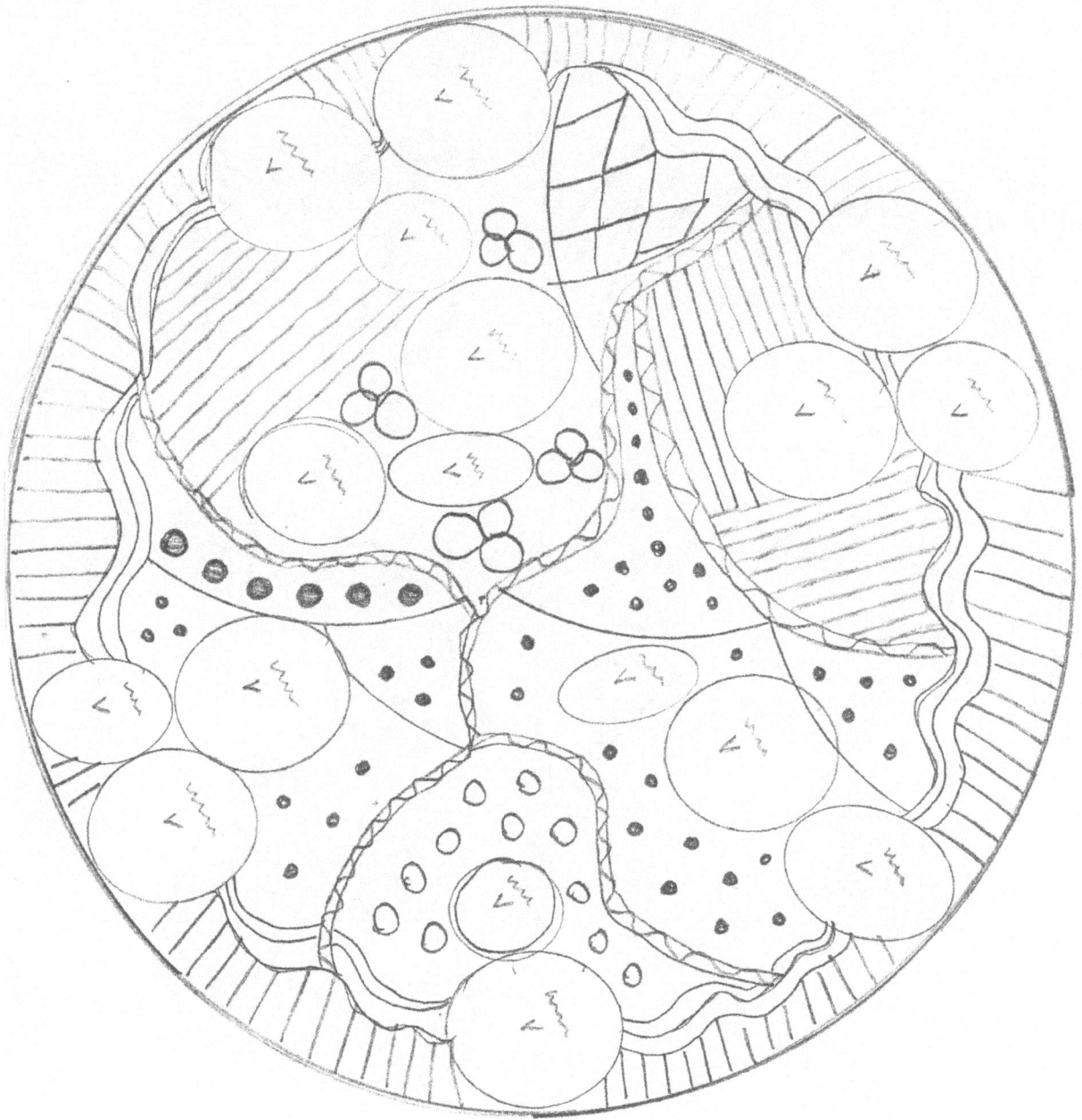

When one door closes
another opens.

Harmony in Life is what we
all strive for.

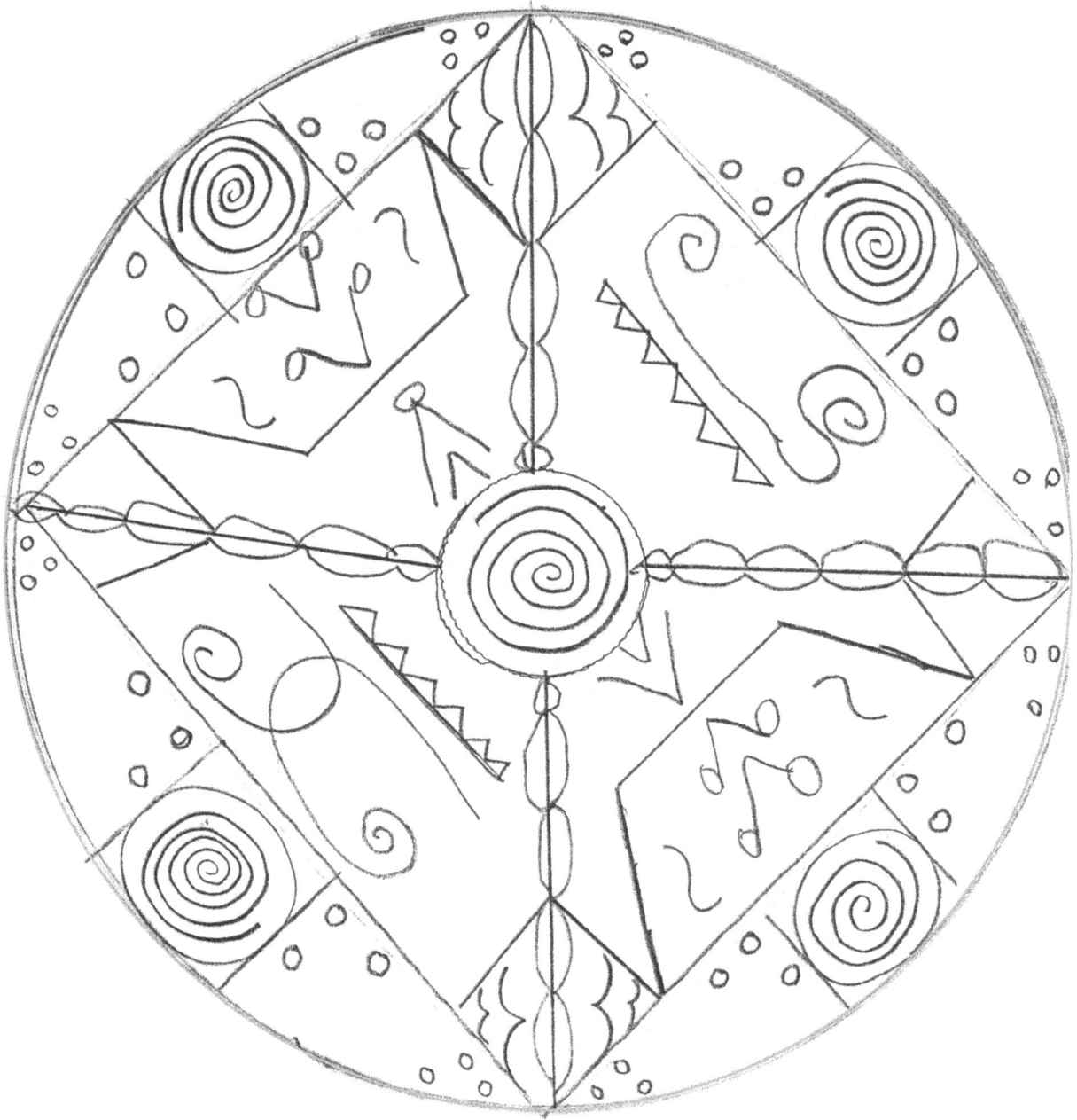

PEACE IS ONLY FOUND THROUGH
LOVE AND COOPERATION.

WE ARE ONE EXPERIENCE OF LIFE AND ONE EXPERIENCE
OF LOVE. TO BE IN HARMONY WITH ALL THERE IS
OPENS INFINITE POSSIBILITIES.

COOPERATION VS. COMPETITION

THE POWER THAT CONTROLS THE UNIVERSE
IS DIVINELY CREATING WITHIN
EACH OF US.

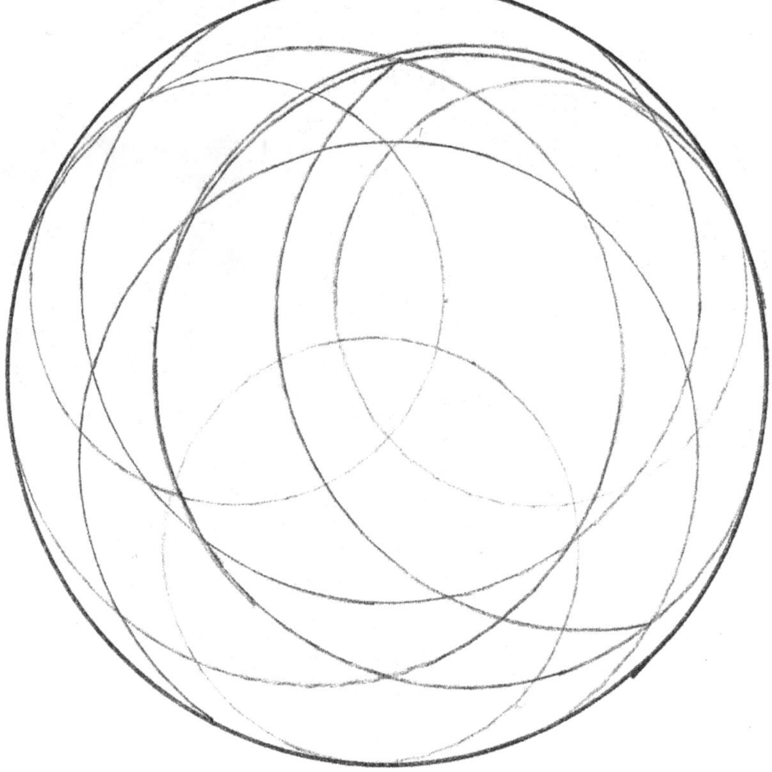

MUTUALLY INCLUSIVE AND MUTUALLY EXCLUSIVE - HOW THEY EXIST IN TANDEM - EACH THE COMPLIMENT OF THE OTHER -
FOREVER MOVING FORWARD AND BEING SO VERY CLOSE AND YET SO VERY FAR - WHAT TO DO?, - EACH IS A WORLD AND WORLD UNTO ITSELF -
COMPLETE AND PROFOUND - EACH SO LONELY WITHOUT THE OTHER FOR CONTRAST AND COMPANY - EACH NEEDING THE OTHER IN CONTRAST -
ALL STRUCTURES ARE UNIFIED - SO THEY STAND - YET SEPARATE IN PERSPECTIVE AND COMPLIMENTIVE QUALITIES - PEACE AND HARMONY ARE
RESONANT NOTES IN A SOMETIMES DISSONANT SONG - ALWAYS COMPLIMENTING THE WHOLE.

ABOUT THE AUTHOR

Ruth Platner's art education began in Hamburg, Germany, her place of birth. She studied at the prestigious *Hamburg Hochschule fur Bildende Künste* under Professor Hans Tietze, where she majored in graphic arts. The school, known for its high standards of excellence, was instrumental in developing Ruth's innate potential. During her twenties, she immigrated to the United States. After raising her three daughters, she enrolled in the University of Wisconsin, where she received a Bachelors degree in Art Education. She subsequently earned a Master's degree in Instructional Technology and embarked upon a teaching career at both the high school and university levels.

Ruth Platner's work reflects her optimistic view of the world and of mankind. She is known for uniquely displaying the elements of vigor and vibrancy throughout her art work. She explains it this way: "All my forms and people are in motion, never static; it is a way to express my personal excitement about living this lifetime of constant change."

In 1997, Ruth Platner founded the Oceanside Museum of Art "School of Art" in Southern California. She served as its director, and was also one of the instructors, until her retirement in 2007. Ruth frequently travels to Trinidad and Tobago in the West Indies, where she enthusiastically shares what she has learned so far, thus keeping herself engaged in her own ongoing evolution.

Ruth's paintings, drawings and textiles have been exhibited at public galleries, exhibits, one-woman shows, juried art shows and art festivals. Her work is collected by art lovers throughout the country.

~ NOTES ~